Essential Physical Science

LIGHT AND SOUND

Louise and Richard Spilsbury

Heinemann
LIBRARY
Chicago, Illinois

Edited by Nancy Dickmann, Adam Miller,
    and Diyan Leake
Designed by Victoria Allen
Original illustrations © Capstone Global
    Library Ltd 2014
Illustrated by H L Studios
Picture research by Ruth Blair
Originated by Capstone Global Library Ltd
Printed in China by CTPS

17 16 15 14 13
10 9 8 7 6 5 4 3 2 1

Library of Congress Cataloging-in-Publication Data
Spilsbury, Louise.-
   Light and sound / Louise and Richard Spilsbury.
      pages cm.—(Essential physical science)
   Includes bibliographical references and index.
   ISBN 978-1-4329-8146-4 (hb)—ISBN 978-1-
4329-8156-3 (pb) 1. Light—Juvenile literature. 2.
Optics—Juvenile literature. 3. Sound—Juvenile
literature. I. Richard, Louise. II. Title.
   QC360.S656 2014
   534—dc23   2012051624

Acknowledgments
We would like to thank the following for
permission to reproduce photographs: Alamy
pp. 8 (© GIPhotoStock X), 15 (© Arcaid Images),
31 (© AfriPics.com), 34 (© Arco Images GmbH),
38 (© Papilio), 39 (© Simon Belcher), 41 (© BSIP
SA), 42 (© Horizon International Images Limited);
Capstone Publishers (© Karon Dubke) pp. 12, 13,
18, 19, 36, 37; Corbis pp. 17 (© Joana Toro/dpa), 21
(© Norbert Wu/Science Faction); Getty Images pp. 9
(Ian Gavan), 23 (Joel Sartore/National Geographic),
25 (Datacraft Co. Ltd), 29 (Dimitri Vervitsiotis), 40
(Visuals Unlimited, Inc./GIPhotoStock); © Anish
Kapoor. All Rights Reserved, DACS 2012 p. 26
(Shutterstock/© gary718); Science Photo Library
pp. 6 (Andrew Lambert Photography), 11 (NASA);
Shutterstock pp. 4 (© egd), 5 (© WindImage), 7
(© Steve Mann), 10 (© melissaf84), 22 (© Monkey
Business Images), 24 (© Angelo Gilardelli),
28 (© MilanB), 33 (© Dmitry Naumov), 35
(© ssuaphotos), 43 (© oorka).

Cover photograph of a trombonist at a festival
reproduced with permission of Superstock
(Cosmo Condina).

Every effort has been made to contact copyright
holders of material reproduced in this book. Any
omissions will be rectified in subsequent printings
if notice is given to the publisher.

Contents

Eureka moment!

Learn about important discoveries that have brought about further knowledge and understanding.

 DID YOU KNOW?

Discover fascinating facts about light and sound.

WHAT'S NEXT?

Read about the latest research and advances in essential physical science.

Some words are shown in bold, **like this**. You can find out what they mean by looking in the glossary.

What Are Light and Sound?

Light and sound are essential to our lives. What would a fireworks display be like without loud bangs, screaming whistles, and brightly colored lights? Sound and light help us enjoy and understand the world around us. They help us to work, play, communicate, and escape from danger. Emergency sirens, such as tornado sirens, are loud, noise-making devices that can warn a whole town about a threat.

Sirens and flashing lights give a clear signal to nearby traffic and pedestrians to pull over and allow police, ambulances, or other emergency vehicles to pass quickly and safely.

Eureka moment!

Steam whistles were an early form of siren. From the 1830s, they were used to send signals on trains and in factories. Steam whistles were also used in lighthouses to warn ships at sea of nearby rocks or hazards.

orms of energy

ound and light are forms of **nergy**. Energy is the ability or power to make things work or happen. Energy can be carried from one place to another. Sunlight is a type of energy that moves from the Sun to Earth. When we speak, the sounds we make are a type of energy that moves from our mouths to people's ears.

▷

DID YOU KNOW?

Without light from the Sun, there would be no life on Earth. Plants use light to grow, and animals cannot live without plants. Animals like us either eat plants or eat animals that eat the plants. Plants also produce most of the **oxygen** we breathe.

Burning gunpowder explodes with a loud banging sound and sends fireworks into the air. Different metals in the gunpowder burn and glow in different colors to create the light displays we see.

How Do We Make Sounds?

Sounds happen when things **vibrate**. When something vibrates, it moves backward and forward or up and down very quickly. This is what happens to the surface of a drum when it is hit with a drumstick. When something vibrates, it makes the air around it vibrate, too. The vibrating air carries the sounds people hear. That is why we stop hearing the sound of a drum when the drummer puts a hand on its surface to prevent it from vibrating.

Feel the vibrations that sounds make by touching your throat when you hum. You can actually see vibrations by putting grain of rice on a drum before you hit it.

Eureka moment!

In 1876, Alexander Graham Bell invented the telephone. When he spoke into his new machine, it changed sound vibrations into **electric currents** that traveled down a wire. At the other end of the wire, the electric currents were changed back into sound vibrations, so his voice could be heard.

How do sounds move?

Sound vibrations travel in invisible patterns called **sound waves**. The waves spread out from a source in all directions, like ripples when you drop a stone in water. Sound waves spread out and pass through gaps or around obstacles, which is why we can hear around corners! When we whisper to someone, we cup our hands around our mouth. This makes a funnel, or cone shape, that helps to focus some of the sound energy in one direction, toward the listener.

Constant noise from airplanes flying over houses near airports can affect residents' sleep, work, and concentration.

Loud and soft

The loudness or softness of sounds depend on the energy in the vibrations. Things that vibrate a lot make a lot of noise! When you hit a drum really hard, you make bigger, stronger vibrations and louder sounds. When you tap a drum or pluck a guitar string gently, you make smaller, weaker vibrations and softer sounds. The farther away you are from a sound, the quieter it gets. This is because sound loses energy as it travels.

Sound waves get taller

Turn up the volume! When you start to hit a drum harder, the vibrations get bigger, the sound waves get taller, and the sounds get louder.

DID YOU KNOW?

One of the loudest natural sounds ever heard came from the eruption of the volcano Krakatoa in Indonesia in 1883. A witness said the explosion still sounded like cannon-fire when it reached him almost 3,100 miles (5,000 kilometers) away. That is like people in Baltimore, Maryland, clearly hearing an explosion that happened all the way in London, England.

Reflecting and absorbing

The space in which a sound is made affects the way it moves, too. Sound waves **reflect**, or bounce off, hard, flat surfaces. That is why we hear **echoes** sometimes, when sound waves reflect back to us from a surface. Soft, bumpy surfaces **absorb** sound waves. Sounds in a room that has carpets, soft seats, and curtains will be different from sounds in an empty room with a wooden floor.

DID YOU KNOW?

The way sound travels in a room is called **acoustics**. Without any echoes in a concert hall, music sounds flat. If there are too many echoes, the music sounds fuzzy. Concert halls are built in special shapes and equipped with panels of different sizes and textures to absorb or reflect sounds, to create the best acoustics for the audience.

What do sounds travel through?

Most of the sounds we hear come to us through the air around us. We may not be able to see air, but air is a **medium**—a material through which sound waves can travel. Sound travels through other mediums, too. It can travel through solids such as metal, stone, and wood, and through liquids such as water.

Sound vibrations travel faster through some mediums than others. For example, sound travels faster through wood than through air. If you get a friend to tap a desk and listen with your head against the desk, the noise will sound louder than it does when you listen in the air.

Sound is an effective way for whales to communicate across deep, dark oceans where they cannot see each other. Blue whales make sounds that can be heard by other whales that are over 500 miles (800 kilometers) away.

DID YOU KNOW?

Sound travels four times faster through water than through air, and it travels 15 times faster through steel than through air.

Sounds in space

Sound always needs a medium to travel through. Sound cannot travel through a **vacuum**—a completely empty space that has nothing in it, not even air. Space is not a perfect vacuum, but there is far too little air in it for sound vibrations to travel through. That is why astronauts can see but not hear each other when they are outside a spacecraft in space.

Eureka moment!

In 1660, the English scientist Robert Boyle discovered that sound waves can only travel if they have a medium to move through. He put an alarm clock in a jar, then pumped out all the air from the jar. Since he could no longer hear the alarm ringing, he had proven that sound needs a medium to travel through.

Astronauts on a space walk need to wear special suits to survive. Even if they did not, they still could not talk or hear each other without radios, because in space there is not enough medium to carry the sound waves.

Try this!

Test three different materials to see how they affect loudness and sound quality (whether sounds are clear or fuzzy).

Prediction

Firmer materials reflect sound better than softer ones.

What you need

- A cardboard box with one open end (ideally over approximately 1 × 1 foot, or 30 × 30 centimeters)
- Sticky tape
- Kraft paper or wallpaper
- Felt or some other thick fabric
- Sponges or pads of foam
- Scissors

What you do

(1) Think of the cardboard box as a room with three walls, a ceiling, and a floor. Get a friend to speak into the open end of the box while you listen behind the other (closed) end of the box. In a normal speaking voice, say, "Hello, how clear and loud does my voice sound now?" to your partner. Switch places and repeat this. Both of you should listen carefully.

(2) Cut the paper into three pieces and stick these to the three inside "walls" of the box with tape, to represent wallpaper. Repeat the speaking sound test that you did in step 1. Is the sound quality and volume different than when there was no paper on the walls of the box? Remove the paper and listen again in the "empty" room.

3 Cut the fabric or felt into three pieces and stick these on the three sides of the box to represent curtains. Try the speaking test again. Do curtains make more difference in the noise level than paper?

4 Tape the sponges to the three sides of the box. These represent sound-absorbing panels. Try the speaking test again. Compare the sound quality and volume to when there were no absorbing panels.

Conclusion

You should have found that paper reflects sound better than the softer materials. Which of the softer materials you tested absorbed the most sound? This was the one in which sounds were softest and fuzziest. Can you think of other materials that would make sounds louder and clearer?

How Do We Hear Sounds?

To hear sounds, our ears detect vibrations made by sound waves. The outer part of the ear acts as a funnel to direct sound waves into the ear. Here, they hit a thin sheet of skin called the eardrum. The sound waves make the eardrum vibrate in a similar way to the original source of the vibration. The eardrum makes three tiny bones (called ossicles) vibrate. These increase the vibrations and pass them into a tube called the cochlea. **Nerves** in the cochlea change vibrations into electrical signals that go to the brain, and we hear the sound. This all happens very quickly.

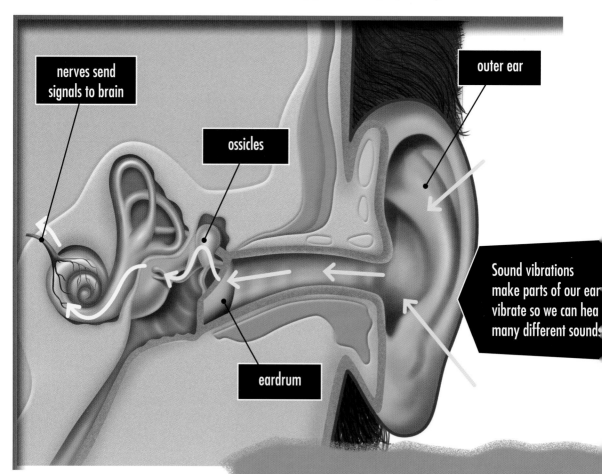

nerves send signals to brain

ossicles

outer ear

Sound vibrations make parts of our ear vibrate so we can hear many different sounds

eardrum

DID YOU KNOW?

You have two ears to tell you which direction sound comes from. The one closest to the sound hears it a bit before and a bit louder than the other. The brain uses this difference to figure out where sounds come from.

Sound signals

The cochlea is lined with 30,000 tiny nerves called hair cells, which look like tiny hairs. Each hair cell picks up and codes different sounds. People may suffer from hearing loss when cochlea hair cells get damaged. For example, very loud sounds can cause vibrations that hit the hair cells so hard they bend or break. Hearing aids called cochlear implants can help people to hear better by changing sounds into electrical signals for them.

Deaf musicians can use sound vibrations to play instruments. Evelyn Glennie removes her boots to make it easier for her to feel the vibrations from her instruments.

WHAT'S NEXT?

A new metal collar may help deaf people enjoy music. It picks up sound vibrations and transmits them directly into a person's skin. This triggers the same sound-processing brain regions as in those with full hearing.

How are high and low sounds made?

We know that loud and quiet sounds are produced by large or small vibrations, but what about high or low sounds, such as a whistle or a lion's roar? High or low sounds are made by fast or slow vibrations. The number of vibrations per second is called the **frequency** of the sound. If you stand on a beach and three waves pass you in a second, the frequency of those waves is three per second. With sound waves, the more frequently or faster something vibrates, the higher the sound it makes.

Eureka moment!

In around 1600, the Italian scientist Galileo discovered that the frequency of sound waves changes how high or low they sound. He noticed that the spacing of the grooves made by a chisel on a brass plate made the sounds of the chisel scraping over it higher or lower.

The low sound of a bass guitar has a low frequency. The high sound of a whistle has a high frequency. The distance between the top of one wave and another is called its **wavelength**.

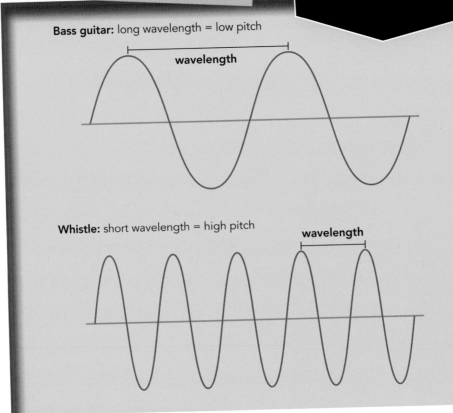

Bass guitar: long wavelength = low pitch

wavelength

Whistle: short wavelength = high pitch

wavelength

Higher and lower

Musicians use the word **pitch** to describe frequency. When the length of a guitar string is changed, it vibrates at a different frequency. A long string gives a lower frequency and pitch. Pressing a finger on it can shorten a string. Shorter strings have a higher frequency and pitch. Blowing into a recorder makes the column of air inside it vibrate and produce sounds. When you put fingers over the holes in a recorder, you change the length of the column of air. The shorter the length of the column of air, the higher the frequency.

▷

DID YOU KNOW?

Young people hear a wider variety of noises than adults. Some ringtones play at such a high pitch that people over the age of 20 cannot hear them!

The longer bars of the marimba make lower notes than the short ones.

Try this!

Investigate how the pitch of a note changes as you change the string's length and tightness.

What you need

- A large, empty can
- A hook
- Modeling clay
- A ruler
- Thin elastic
- A plastic bottle
- Weights (small enough to fit inside the bottle, such as marbles)

What you do

1 Push or hammer the hook into the lid of the can, near one edge.

2 Use the modeling clay to attach the ruler to the opposite edge of the can. It should be standing on one of its short edges.

3 Cut a strip of elastic about 3 feet (1 meter) long. Tie one end around the hook and the other to the top of the plastic bottle. Stand the can near the edge of a table, then put a weight into the bottle and hang it over the edge of the ruler.

4 Pluck the elastic (this is like the string of your instrument) with your finger. Listen carefully to the note it makes and how high or low it sounds.

5 Put another weight into the bottle and pluck the string again. What difference does this make? Try this a few more times. How does the note change as the string gets longer and tighter?

Conclusion

Looser strings make lower notes. When weights pull on the string, they tighten it. Tightening a string gives it a higher pitch (or frequency), while loosening it lowers the frequency. When string players tighten or loosen their strings, they are altering the pitches to make them in tune.

Stay safe!

Make sure the can does not have any jagged edges that could scratch you, and don't pluck the elastic too hard, in case it snaps up and hits you in the eye.

How Do We Use Sound?

Sound is used in many ways in science and industry. **Sonar** devices are used to find and locate objects under the sea. Sonar machines send out sound waves. When the waves hit an object, echoes are reflected off it. The machine then analyzes the echoes. By figuring out the direction of returning echoes and measuring the time taken for them to return, the sonar machine can give precise information about the direction, size, and position of the object.

The word *sonar* is an abbreviation for *so*und, *na*vigation, and *r*anging. People use sonar to map the shape and features of the ocean floor.

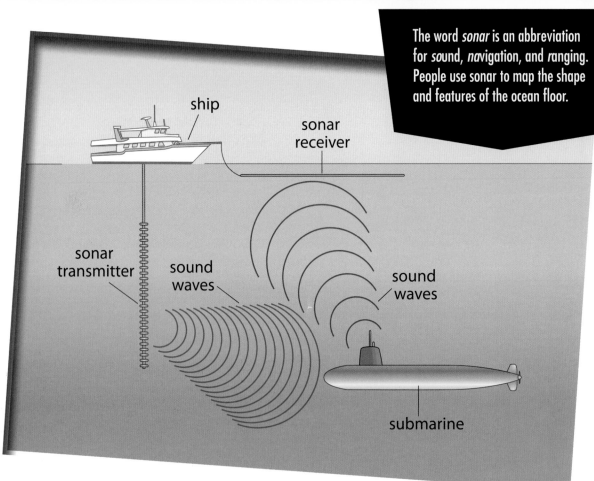

ship

sonar receiver

sonar transmitter

sound waves

sound waves

submarine

Eureka moment!

Lewis Nixon invented the very first sonar-type listening device in 1906, as a way for ships to detect icebergs.

Using sonar

Sonar has many uses. Fishing boats use sonar equipment to locate schools of fish. Naval ships detect enemy submarines and mines using sonar. Sonar can also be used to find shipwrecks and to measure water depths. Some scientists use sonar to explore underground. They send sound waves into the ground. Then they study the echoes that reflect off layers of rock underground, to identify those that might be worth drilling into to find useful gas, oil, or other **minerals**.

DID YOU KNOW?

Dolphins and porpoises use a type of sonar called **echolocation** to find animals to eat. They send out high-frequency sounds and then use the echoes from possible prey to figure out their type, location, speed, and direction of movement.

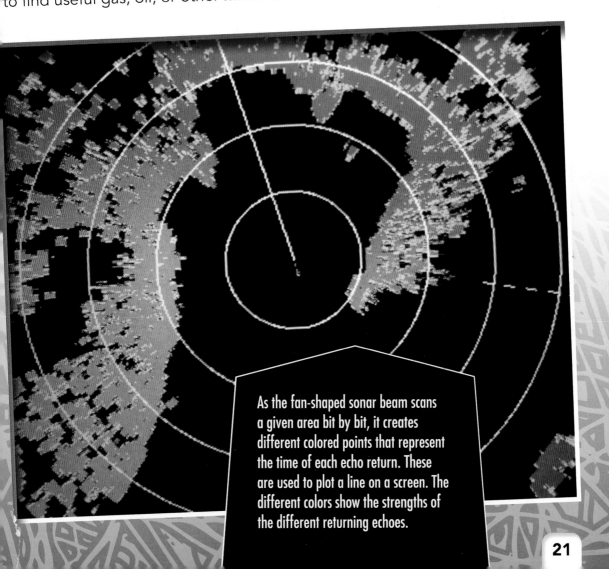

As the fan-shaped sonar beam scans a given area bit by bit, it creates different colored points that represent the time of each echo return. These are used to plot a line on a screen. The different colors show the strengths of the different returning echoes.

Ultrasound machines

Doctors in hospitals use a special kind of sonar equipment called **ultrasound**. An ultrasound machine uses sound waves of a very high frequency that produces different echoes when reflected by different **organs** inside the body, such as the heart and liver. Doctors can use these echoes to detect cancerous **tumors** and diseases such as liver disease. Doctors also use ultrasound to scan unborn babies inside their mother's body, so they can monitor the babies' growth and health.

WHAT'S NEXT?

In the future, hospitals may be equipped with ultrasound devices that produce highly focused sound waves. These can be used to break up bloo clots in the brain or destroy diseased brain tissue without the need for surgery or drugs

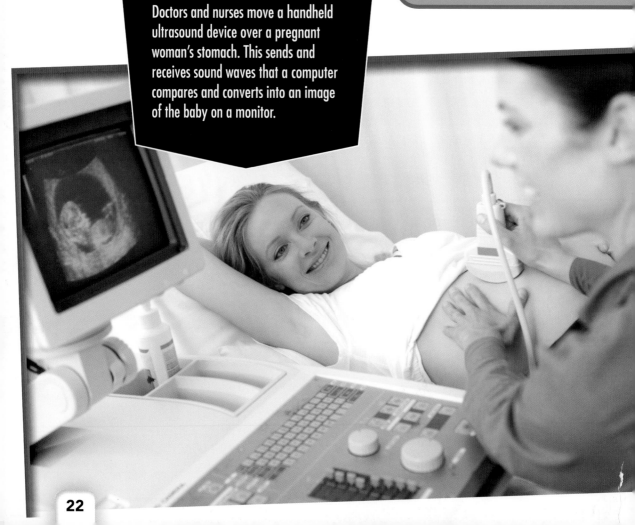

Doctors and nurses move a handheld ultrasound device over a pregnant woman's stomach. This sends and receives sound waves that a computer compares and converts into an image of the baby on a monitor.

Ultrasonic waves

Since the 1950s, ultrasonic waves have been used to clean delicate machinery parts—for example, to dislodge very tiny pieces of dirt or other matter from aircraft. Today, ultrasound is also used to clean objects such as watches and jewelry. Manufacturers use ultrasonic waves to test the quality of metals, plastics, and other materials in the things they make. Some dentists use ultrasonic waves to clean teeth—and today you can even buy ultrasonic toothbrushes!

DID YOU KNOW?

Bats use ultrasound to hunt prey. The sound waves they produce are very close together, so they can detect the very small prey that they prefer, such as moths. Dolphins make sound waves farther apart to find larger prey, including fish.

How Does Light Move?

Light is similar to sound in some ways. Light and sound are both forms of energy, and they both carry energy in the form of waves. Like sound, light moves in waves away from its source. However, unlike sound, light tries to move in straight lines that we call **rays**.

An object that gives off light—for example, the Sun, a lamp, or a computer screen—is **luminous**. The Sun is our most important natural source of light. We manufacture most of the other luminous objects we use. A flashlight bulb glows because electricity heats a wire inside it, and a candle gives off light as its wick burns.

When a cloud moves in front of the Sun in the sky, we can sometimes see rays of sunlight shining from behind.

WHAT'S NEXT?

Scientists are working on "living lamps" made of glass jars filled with **bacteria** that give off a green glow when fed with methane gas. Methane is produced by rotting household waste—so, one day, we could have natural light in our homes and reduce waste at the same time!

Transparent and opaque

Unlike sound, light waves can move through a vacuum. That is why sunlight can travel through space from the Sun to Earth. However, light cannot move through everything. Light can move through **transparent** materials, such as glass, air, and water, but it cannot pass through **opaque** things, such as walls, trees, and us! When opaque materials stop light from passing through them, shadows form on the other side of them, where the light cannot reach. Some things are **translucent**—for example, the **lenses** in dark glasses. Translucent materials let some, but not all, of the light pass through them.

DID YOU KNOW?

Light moves faster than anything else in the universe. Light is a million times faster than sound. Light from the Sun takes only eight minutes to travel 93 million miles (150 million kilometers) to Earth. This means that we see the sunset eight minutes after it actually happened.

The tennis player casts a shadow in bright sunlight, but the shadow of the racket head is lighter than other parts. This is because, although the strings are opaque, light shines through holes between them.

Reflecting and absorbing light

When light cannot pass through an object, it reacts in different ways. Some of the waves are reflected, or bounce back off the surface of the object. Some waves are absorbed. Dark surfaces absorb more light than they reflect, and light surfaces reflect more light than they absorb. Smooth, flat surfaces reflect light best. When light hits a mirror or the metal roof of a car, its rays bounce off in only one direction, like a bouncing ball.

Mirrors reflect light efficiently because they are very smooth and shiny.

▷ DID YOU KNOW?

There is no such thing as moonlight! Only stars, such as our Sun, are luminous and make light. The light of the Moon is actually a reflection of the light from the Sun. So, on a moonlit night, we're actually getting sunlight that is bouncing off the Moon.

Scattering light

Most surfaces are not completely smooth and flat when you look at them up close. When light shines on a surface such as a tree or concrete, its waves bounce off in lots of different directions. This is called **scattering**. Scattering is how sunlight lights up Earth. When waves of sunlight hit tiny **particles** of dust in the **atmosphere**, the light is scattered in all directions so that its light spreads all around. It is dark in space because there is no atmosphere there to scatter light from the stars.

WHAT'S NEXT?

In the future, we may be able to buy invisibility cloaks! Scientists are developing thin, film-like materials that can interrupt the flow of light and channel it around objects, rather than being absorbed or reflected by it. This will make the object appear invisible.

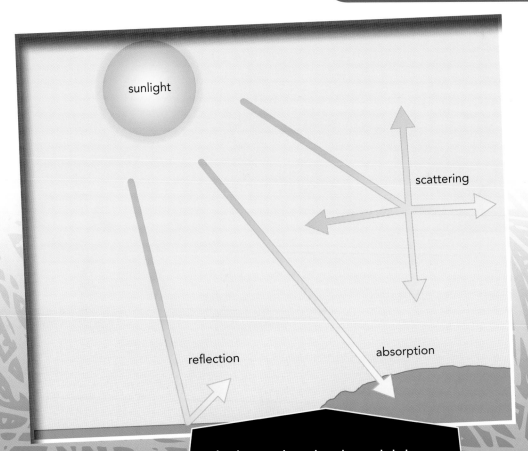

sunlight

scattering

reflection

absorption

This diagram shows that when sunlight hits a surface, it can be absorbed or reflected, but it can also be scattered by particles in the atmosphere before reaching the surface.

Refraction

Light can also bend. Have you ever noticed how a straw looks bent in a glass of water, or how a swimming pool looks shallower than it really is? These effects are caused by **refraction**, which is the way light bends when it passes through something. Refraction happens because light travels at different speeds through different things. It moves faster through air than through water. Light slows down by about 25 percent when it moves from air to water. As it slows down, it changes its direction—it bends, or refracts.

The straw looks bent because light slows down when it moves from air to water.

Moving through mediums

Light, like sound, can travel through different mediums. When light shines into glass, water, or plastic, it also refracts. The amount the light bends depends on the type of medium it travels through. For example, light moves more slowly through glass than through water, so light refracts more when moving through glass than when moving through water.

DID YOU KNOW?
Archerfish use their mouth like a water gun, shooting water out to knock insects off branches into the water. To aim accurately, they have to allow for refraction, and they have learned that there is less distortion of their vision of the target if they position themselves directly beneath it.

When light hits a diamond, some of it reflects back, but some travels into the center of the diamond and bounces around inside before finally escaping. This makes the diamond sparkle.

How Does Light Help Us to See?

We can only see because of light. We see when light reflects off an object and enters our eyes. Light enters the eye through the black spot in the middle called the pupil. It passes through a cornea and a lens, which both help to focus light onto the **retina** at the back of the eyeball. The retina is covered in nerve cells that send signals down the optic nerve to the brain. The brain turns these signals into the image that we see.

The image passed to the retina is upside-down. The brain turns it the right way up again.

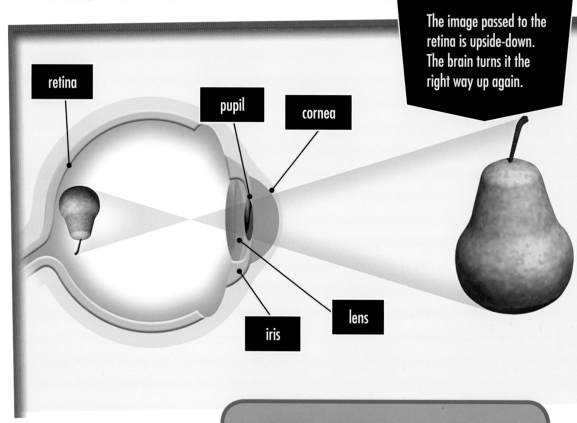

retina

pupil

cornea

lens

iris

WHAT'S NEXT?

A new, artificial retina could help blind people to see. A video camera in a pair of glasses records scenes and sends beams of light onto a computer chip at the back of the eyeball. This creates electrical signals that pass directly into the optic nerve.

Changing light

Our eyes are constantly changing to control how much light gets into them and to focus on different things. The **iris**, the colored part of the eye, is a circle of muscle that changes the size of the pupil. In bright light, eyes need to take in less light to be able to see, so it makes the pupil smaller. In low light, it makes the pupil bigger, to take in more light. Other muscles change the shape of the lens to make it focus on things near and far.

Cats' eyes seem to glow when light shines on them. This is because they reflect light inside, to help them see!

DID YOU KNOW?

Cats can see in low light because of a mirror-like part at the back of their eyes called the *tapetum lucidum*. This reflects any light that is not absorbed by the retina. The reflected light is bounced back, so the retina has another chance to absorb it.

How do glasses help us see?

People who are nearsighted cannot see things at a distance clearly. Their lenses focus the image in front of the retina. People who are farsighted see things far away clearly, but their near vision is blurry. Their lenses focus the image behind the retina. Some people wear glasses to help them see more clearly if the lenses in their eyes do not refract light onto the retina properly. The lenses in glasses are curved, in order to refract light so it hits the retina again.

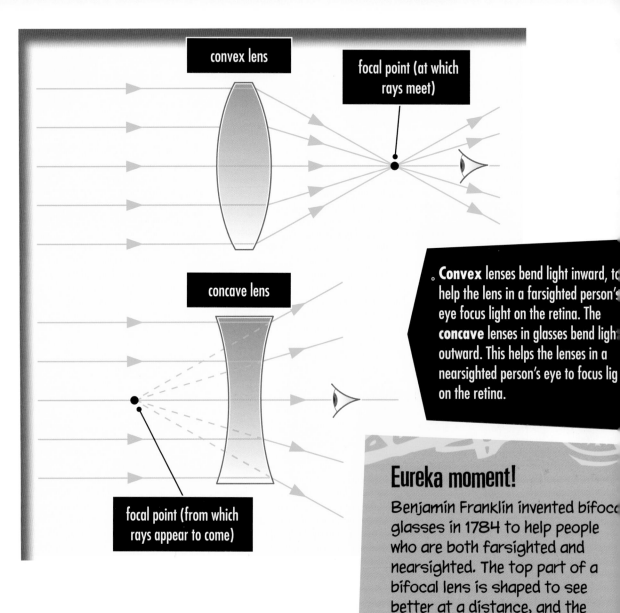

convex lens

focal point (at which rays meet)

concave lens

focal point (from which rays appear to come)

Convex lenses bend light inward, to help the lens in a farsighted person's eye focus light on the retina. The **concave** lenses in glasses bend light outward. This helps the lenses in a nearsighted person's eye to focus light on the retina.

Eureka moment!

Benjamin Franklin invented bifocal glasses in 1784 to help people who are both farsighted and nearsighted. The top part of a bifocal lens is shaped to see better at a distance, and the bottom part is curved to see better up close.

Contact lenses

Contact lenses are also curved lenses that refract light to help people see, worn directly on the surface of the eye. Tears on the surface of the eyes help to hold them in place. A Swiss doctor named Adolf Fick made the first contact lenses in 1887 from glass. They were large and heavy, and they covered the entire eye surface, so they were very uncomfortable to wear! Today's contact lenses are made from thin, soft, flexible plastic and only cover the iris, so wearers cannot feel them.

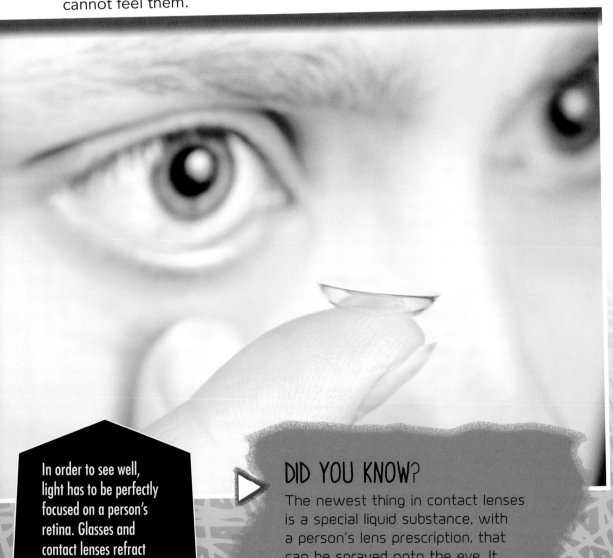

In order to see well, light has to be perfectly focused on a person's retina. Glasses and contact lenses refract light so that it hits a person's retina correctly.

DID YOU KNOW?

The newest thing in contact lenses is a special liquid substance, with a person's lens prescription, that can be sprayed onto the eye. It hardens into a contact lens that lasts for up to 24 hours.

How do we see colors?

Light seems to be colorless, but in fact it is made up of different colored waves. Each color has a different wavelength. For example, violet light has a shorter wavelength than red light. Objects are a particular color when they reflect one wavelength and absorb others. For example, a ripe tomato looks bright red because its skin reflects the red light in sunlight and absorbs all other colors. An object appears black when it absorbs all wavelengths, and white when it reflects all wavelengths.

When light waves pass through water droplets that have many sides, it splits into its different colors: red, orange, yellow, green, blue, indigo, and violet.

Eureka moment!

In 1666, Isaac Newton discovered that white light is made up of different colors when he shone a beam of sunlight through a **prism**. A prism is a wedge of glass that refracts light and splits it into its different colors.

Why is the sky blue?

On a clear day, the sky looks blue because of the way Earth's atmosphere scatters light from the Sun. As sunlight travels through the atmosphere toward Earth, it is scattered in all directions by gases and particles in the air. Blue light is scattered more than other colors because it travels as shorter, smaller waves. That is why we see a blue sky most of the time. As the Sun gets lower in the sky, its light has to pass through more of the atmosphere to reach Earth. This means that more of the blue light is scattered, which lets other colors—the reds and yellows of a sunset—reach your eyes.

We see blue skies when particles in the atmosphere absorb and scatter more blue light than other colors.

Try this!

Raindrops and prisms can split white light into the seven colors of the rainbow. But did you know that you can reverse the process by mixing the seven colors together to make white light? You can find out how this is done by making a rainbow spinner.

What you need:

- White cardboard
- Scissors
- A cup
- A cutting mat or mousepad
- A piece of strong string about 48 inches (120 centimeters) long
- A protractor (optional)
- Colored pencils or markers in red, orange, yellow, green, blue, indigo, and violet
- A pencil

What you do

1 Use the cup to draw a neat circle on the white cardboard. Cut out this circle.

2 Divide the circle into seven equal segments. (You can use the protractor to help you do this, if you know how.)

36

3 Color the segments the seven colors of the rainbow: red, orange, yellow, green, blue, indigo, and violet.

4 Rest the cardboard circle on the mat. Push a pencil through the cardboard in two places to make two holes in the center, about ⅓ inch (1 centimeter) apart.

5 Thread the string through the two holes and tie it so there is a loop at each end.

6 To spin your rainbow spinner, put one finger through the end of each loop and flip the disc over the string several times, until the string has lots of twists in it. Pull your hands apart to tighten the string, and then let the string go slack. If you do this properly, the disc should spin. What color does the cardboard look when it spins fast?

Conclusion
When the disc is still, white light is reflected and absorbed by the different segments, so we see separate rainbow colors. When the disc spins quickly, your brain does not have enough time to see the colors differently. Instead, it detects an overall mix of the colors, so the disc looks white or off-white.

How Do We Use Light?

We use light in many different devices. We can use it to take photos, carry signals, and cut materials. By reflecting and refracting light in different ways, we can use it to see faraway objects and to make very tiny things visible.

Microscopes and telescopes

A compound microscope shines light through two sets of lenses to magnify very small objects on a slide, in order to make them visible. A refracting telescope is a tube with a lens at each end. The first lens forms an image, and the second lens makes the image look bigger. In a reflecting telescope, the image is formed by reflection from a curved mirror that is then magnified by a second mirror.

Microscopes use lenses or mirrors to help us see tiny objects close up. Fifty of these tiny marine animals end to end would measure about ⅓ inch (1 centimeter).

Eureka moment!

In 1609, the Italian scientist Galileo made an improved version of previous attempts at making telescopes. His telescope boosted the viewing power enough for him to get a good look at the Moon.

Digital cameras

Digital cameras use light to make photos. Light enters the camera through a lens, as it does through an eye—but the light in the camera hits a sensor rather than a retina. The sensor detects the light and sends electrical signals to a microchip. The microchip processes and pieces together the information into an image that we can view on a screen.

This is the view a pilot has on a screen in the cockpit of an airplane when flying at night using a night-vision camera.

WHAT'S NEXT?

Night-vision goggles bounce infrared light (a type of light we cannot see) off a special screen to make a green or red image we can see. Previously, the screens were made from heavy glass, and the goggles were expensive to produce. Scientists have found a way to construct much thinner goggles using cheap, lightweight plastic and other materials. In the future, the same technology might make night-vision glasses and night-vision car windshields common.

Laser light

Laser is a special form of light that is made by machines. Laser light is made up of only one type of wavelength (or color) of light. The light waves travel **parallel** to each other in the same direction and do not scatter in the atmosphere. Laser beams are therefore very narrow and can be concentrated onto one spot to produce a small point of intense energy. This makes lasers useful as cutting tools as well as other things.

Eureka moment!

After their moonwalk in 1969, astronauts Buzz Aldrin and Neil Armstrong left a set of mirrors on the Moon. The mirrors reflect laser pulses sent from Earth, so that scientists can precisely measure the distance from Earth to the Moon. We now know that the Moon is drifting 1½ inches (3.8 centimeters) away from Earth every year.

Some lasers are used to write and read CDs and DVDs.

Lasers can permanently change the shape of the cornea and improve patients' eyesight.

Using lasers

Lasers carry TV and telephone signals through special cables. Metalworkers use lasers to cut and weld metal into a wide range of things, including cars. In clothing factories, lasers can cut through hundreds of layers of fabric at once. Lasers are also used in bar-code readers in stores. Because laser light travels in a straight line, it can be used for many types of alignment and measurement.

In surgery, lasers are sometimes used instead of scalpels because they can cut skin cleanly and precisely. They are especially useful in delicate eye surgery, where they are used to change the shape of the cornea, so that it focuses light on the retina correctly.

WHAT'S NEXT?

Scientists have created a gadget that seals up flesh wounds with a quick zap of a laser. Could this be the end for surgical stitches?

How Can We Take Care of Our Eyes and Ears?

Light and sound are essential to our lives. It's important to protect our eyes and ears, so we can continue using and experiencing light and sound to our best ability.

Protecting ears

The loudness of sound is measured in decibels (dB). On decibel is the smallest sound we can hear. We speak at abo 60 dB, and a clap of thunder can be 120 dB. Sounds of 85 dB or more can permanent damage ears—especially if they go on for a long time. It is important not to have the volume on your earphones set too loud or to stand too close to speakers at concerts.

People who work with noisy machinery for long periods protect their ears to avoid damaging their hearing.

DID YOU KNOW?

The sound of a jet aircraft taking off is about 120 dB. Pilots wear special headphones to protect their hearing. These headphones analyze the noise and then produce sound waves exactly opposite in shape, which cancel out the noise of the aircraft.

Protecting eyes

The retinas in our eyes can be damaged by very bright light, so it is important to wear wide-brimmed hats and good-quality sunglasses on sunny days. Some people wear goggles to protect their eyes when playing sports. Wearing goggles when playing racquetball protects eyes from being hit by high-speed balls. Ski goggles prevent eye damage from sunlight reflecting off snow.

When we stare at a computer screen for a long time, we tend not to blink. This makes our eyes dry and tired, which is why we should take regular breaks. It is also important to get regular checkups at the eye doctor.

Eureka moment!

Inuit people made some of the earliest sunglasses from bone, leather, or wood with small slits to see through, to protect their eyes from the bright sunlight that reflects off snow.

Even when there is an exciting event like a solar eclipse — when the Moon passes in front of the Sun — we should *never* look directly toward the Sun.

Glossary

absorb take something in. For example, a sponge absorbs water.

acoustics way that sound travels in a confined space such as a room or theater

atmosphere layer of gases that surround Earth

bacteria living things that are too small to be seen without a microscope

concave curving in toward the center

convex curving outward on each side

echo sound caused by the reflection of sound waves from a surface back to the listener

echolocation way of finding objects and visualizing surroundings in the dark using reflected sound waves

electric current flow or movement of electricity

energy ability or power to do work

frequency number of vibrations per second

iris thin structure in eyes that controls how much light enters through the pupil and strikes the lens and retina inside. The iris is also the colored part of the eye.

laser device that gives out a narrow, powerful beam of light, made up of a single wavelength or color

lens in an eye, the clear part that focuses light rays on the retina. An artificial lens is a transparent object that refracts (bends) light in useful ways.

luminous gives out its own light

medium material through which sound or light waves can travel

mineral substance such as oil or metal that is found in the ground

nerve fiber that carries messages between the brain and the rest of the body, allowing us to do things such as see, hear, and feel pain

opaque material through which light cannot pass

organ important body part such as the heart or liver

oxygen gas in the air that animals need to breathe in order to live

parallel when something is parallel to something else, the two things are side by side and have the same distance between them

particle extremely tiny piece of material

pitch how high or low a sound is

prism piece of glass with triangular ends that splits light into its separate colors

ray straight path or beam of light

reflect bend or throw back light

refraction way light rays bend when they pass at an angle from one kind of material (such as water) to another (such as air)

retina layer at the back of the eyeball that is sensitive to light and sends signals to the brain about what we see

scattering when waves reflect or bounce off something in lots of different directions

sonar machine that uses the echoes of ultrasound waves to detect things underwater or underground

sound wave vibration in a medium such as air or water that we hear as sound

supersonic faster than the speed of sound

translucent something that lets some but not all light pass through it

transparent material through which light passes easily, such as clear glass

tumor mass of cells growing in a part of the body where they should not be

ultrasound high-frequency sound waves making sounds outside the range of normal human hearing

vacuum completely empty space with nothing in it, not even air

vibrate move forward and backward or up and down, quickly and repeatedly

wavelength distance between two crests of a wave

Find out more

Books

Dicker, Katie. *Light* (Sherlock Bones Looks at Physical Science). New York: Windmill, 2011.

McGregor, Harriet. *Sound* (Sherlock Bones Looks at Physical Science). New York: Windmill, 2011.

Walker, Sally M. *Investigating Light* (Searchlight Books: How Does Energy Work?). Minneapolis: Lerner, 2012.

Walker, Sally M. *Investigating Sound* (Searchlight Books: How Does Energy Work?). Minneapolis: Lerner, 2012.

Web sites

www.brainpopjr.com/science/energy/light/preview.weml
Learn more about light at BrainPOP's site.

www.brainpop.com/science/energy/sound/preview.weml
Learn more about sound at BrainPOP's site.

coolcosmos.ipac.caltech.edu
On this web site, you can learn more about the amazing world of infrared and other wavelengths of light.

pbskids.org/zoom/activities/sci/#sound
Try different science experiments relating to sound on this PBS web site.

Places to visit

Exploratorium
Pier 15
San Francisco, California 94111
www.exploratorium.edu
This museum examines many different aspects of science, including light and sound, and offers hands-on activities.

Museum of Science and Industry
5700 S. Lake Shore Drive
Chicago, Illinois 60637
www.msichicago.org
This museum includes exhibits relating to light and sound, including an interactive color booth and a "whispering gallery" that explores sound waves.

Further research

Find out more about how a mirror reflects all the light that hits it to give such good reflections. How do two-way mirrors work, and where are they useful?

Many animals use colored patterns in their skin as camouflage. Cuttlefish, octopuses, and chameleons are among those that can change color as they move across different-colored backgrounds and to communicate. Research how they do this.

A saxophone, an electric guitar, a trumpet, and a tabla drum make music in different ways. Find out how each makes vibrations and what parts make the sound louder. Then search for a piece of music featuring each instrument that you like!

Index